ANIMAL INVADERS: DESTROYING NATIVE HABITATS

ATTACK OF THE ASIAN CARP

BY SANTANA HUNT

Gareth Stevens PUBLISHING

Please visit our website, www.garethstevens.com. For a free color catalog of all our high-quality books, call toll free 1-800-542-2595 or fax 1-877-542-2596.

Cataloging-in-Publication Data

Names: Hunt, Santana.
Title: Attack of the Asian carp / Santana Hunt.
Description: New York : Gareth Stevens Publishing, 2017. | Series: Animal invaders: destroying native habitats | Includes index.
Identifiers: ISBN 9781482456554 (pbk.) | ISBN 9781482456936 (library bound) | ISBN 9781482456912 (6 pack)
Subjects: LCSH: Introduced aquatic organisms–Juvenile literature. | Biological invasions–Juvenile literature. | Environmental disasters–Juvenile literature.
Classification: LCC QH90.8.I57 H83 2017 | DDC 578.6'2–dc23

First Edition

Published in 2017 by
Gareth Stevens Publishing
111 East 14th Street, Suite 349
New York, NY 10003

Designer: Laura Bowen
Editor: Kristen Nelson

Photo credits: Cover, pp. 1 (carp) Vladimir Wrangel/Shutterstock.com; cover, pp. 1–24 (background) arigato/Shutterstock.com; cover, pp. 1–24 (corners) Gala/Shutterstock.com; cover, pp. 1–24 (title bar) drada/Shutterstock.com; pp. 1–24 (caption box) Amovitania/Shutterstock.com; p. 5 Wichita Eagle/Tribune News Service/Getty Images; p. 7 ullstein bild/Getty Images; p. 9 (silver) Etrusko25/Wikimedia Commons; p. 9 (bighead) Nonchanon/Shutterstock.com; p. 9 (grass) FEXX/Wikimedia Commons; p. 9 (black) Quibik/Wikimedia Commons; p. 11 jubipulse34/Shutterstock.com; p. 13 (red plankton) Micha/Wikimedia Commons; p. 13 (purple plankton) Biopics/Wikimedia Commons; p. 13 (blue plankton) Uwe kils/Wikimedia Commons; pp. 15, 21 (map) kateukraine/Shutterstock.com; p. 17 (upper inset) Svetlana Ageeva/Shutterstock.com; pp. 17 (lower inset), 19 Scott Olson/Getty Images News/Getty Images.

Printed in the United States of America

CPSIA compliance information: Batch #CW17GS: For further information contact Gareth Stevens, New York, New York at 1-800-542-2595.

CONTENTS

Words in the glossary appear in **bold** type the first time they are used in the text.

LEAPING ONTO THE SCENE

For many people, fishing is relaxing and fun. But imagine turning on your boat's motor and a huge fish flies out of the water into your face! That's just one way Asian carp are making their mark on some waterways in the United States.

"Asian carp" is a general name for several species, or kinds, of carp native to China, Russia, and other parts of eastern Asia. Asian carp in the United States include the grass carp, black carp, bighead carp, and silver carp.

FIGHT BACK WITH FACTS

Asian carp are invasive species, which are living things likely to spread and be harmful to native animals and plants when put into a new habitat.

The silver carp is the kind that jumps out of the water. Boat motors and other loud sounds **startle** the fish, and it can jump up to 10 feet (3 m) in the air!

BROUGHT TO HELP

Catfish farmers brought Asian carp to the southern United States during the 1960s and 1970s. The fish were meant to stop the growth of harmful plants, **algae**, and other pests in fish farms, ponds, and lakes.

However, some Asian carp escaped when floods raised water levels enough for them to swim—or jump—out of the ponds and lakes to waterways that led to the Mississippi River. Fishermen also started the spread of Asian carp by using baby Asian carp as bait.

FIGHT BACK WITH FACTS

Asian carp have been raised in Asia for more than 1,000 years!

Asian carp were known to be invasive in other parts of the world, including Australia. Maybe the fish farmers should have been more careful—or not introduced them at all!

BIG FISH

Asian carp are a silvery color, though each species' body looks a little different. Some of the difference is in size. Bighead carp can be about 5 feet (1.5 m) long and grow to be more than 100 pounds (45 kg)! Grass carp can grow to be almost as big. Silver carp and black carp are smaller, weighing only about 60 to 70 pounds (27 to 32 kg) at most.

Bighead and silver carp eat **plankton**. Black carp eat snails and mussels.

FIGHT BACK WITH FACTS

Asian carp like to live in large rivers with somewhat warm waters.

The grass carp can eat up to 40 percent of its body weight in plants each day.

GRASS CARP

BIGHEAD CARP

SILVER CARP

BLACK CARP

A GROWING POPULATION

Like other fish, Asian carp **reproduce** by laying eggs. Adult carp like to live in slow-moving water, but they look for fast-moving water to **spawn**. This allows the eggs to spread quickly.

A female Asian carp lays eggs a few times a year. Each time, she may lay hundreds of thousands of eggs! While not all the larvae that hatch from these eggs will live to be adults, Asian carp are still reproducing at a much higher rate than native fish.

FIGHT BACK WITH FACTS

It's hard to know how many Asian carp are in a body of water. Nets used to catch fish for counting often aren't strong enough to hold them, or they jump out of the nets!

Because they aren't native fish, Asian carp don't have many predators. There's nothing in their new habitat to keep their populations in check.

GREEDY FEEDERS

A growing population of nonnative fish with big **appetites** can cause a lot of harm to the habitats they live in.

Of the four species of Asian carp, the silver carp and bighead carp are the most **threatening**. Each fish may eat as much as 20 percent of its body weight in plankton a day! Plankton is an important source of food for many native fish and mussels. Without it, their populations will fall, and the **ecosystem** will become unbalanced.

FIGHT BACK WITH FACTS

Asian carp need to eat so much because their stomachs don't break down food very well.

Asian carp not only reproduce more, but also grow faster than native fish. Bigger Asian carp need more food, like this plankton!

SPREAD TO THE NORTH

Every year since they escaped the fish farms, Asian carp have spread. They moved upstream in the Mississippi River through **locks**. Boats traveling waterways where Asian carp lived picked up young Asian carp or eggs, dropping them in other bodies of water.

Many worry Asian carp will reach the Great Lakes. The Great Lakes fishing industry makes billions of dollars each year. Asian carp could seriously harm the Great Lakes ecosystem and cost the industry a lot of money.

FIGHT BACK WITH FACTS

A group called the Great Lakes Commission has been studying the spread of Asian carp for years and working to keep these fish out of the Great Lakes.

The Chicago Sanitary and Ship Canal connects the Great Lakes to the Mississippi River. That's the waterway many people fear Asian carp will use to reach the Great Lakes.

SHOCKER!

Closing down the Chicago Sanitary and Ship Canal may be the only way to stop Asian carp from entering the Great Lakes. However, this waterway is used for millions of dollars of shipping every year.

In 2002, the US Army Corps of Engineers built the first electric **barriers** to keep Asian carp away from Lake Michigan, where the canal enters the Great Lakes. So far, only one Asian carp has made it past these barriers, and it was caught before it reached the lake.

FIGHT BACK WITH FACTS

The electricity from the barriers could stop a human heart! Can it stop Asian carp from spreading?

Closing the Chicago Sanitary and Ship Canal would mean lost jobs and money for the nearby area. Even more might be lost should Asian carp enter the Great Lakes, though. The Asian carp problem in Australia costs the country $400 million a year!

CHICAGO RIVER

CHICAGO SANITARY AND SHIP CANAL

SCIENCE TO THE RESCUE?

Science might have the answer to stopping Asian carp. One study says Asian carp stay away from water that has added gas in it. Other scientists are trying to find an illness that might kill a lot of Asian carp at once. Adding **chemicals** to the water that would kill Asian carp is another idea some are looking into.

Some of these plans might work. But it's important to find out how they will affect other wildlife and water quality.

FIGHT BACK WITH FACTS

Adding the gas carbon dioxide to water makes the water bubbly like soda!

These men are adding chemicals to a short part of Little Calumet River in Illinois to kill the fish there. This will help them see if any Asian carp live there.

EAT THEM

Did you know you can eat Asian carp? Carp isn't a popular food fish in the United States, but many people in Asia like it!

Instead of focusing on stopping the spread of Asian carp, some people want to simply make use of the overpopulation. One chef in Louisiana has figured out how to clean the fish well and wants to set up a place to **process** the fish in order to sell it. He calls the idea "Can't Beat 'Em. Eat 'Em."

This map shows where all kinds of Asian carp have been found. It includes grass carp, the least threatening species that has spread the furthest.

SPREAD OF THE ASIAN CARP

GLOSSARY

algae: plantlike living things that are mostly found in water

appetite: a wish to eat when food is present

barrier: something that makes traveling hard

chemical: matter added to other matter to cause changes

ecosystem: all the living things in an area

habitat: the natural place where an animal or plant lives

lock: a device for raising and lowering ships between stretches of water that are different levels

plankton: a tiny plant or animal that floats in a body of water

process: to prepare

reproduce: when an animal creates another creature just like itself

spawn: a way some marine animals reproduce in which eggs are let loose in the water

startle: to move or jump when scared or surprised

threatening: giving signs as something that could cause harm

FOR MORE INFORMATION

Books

Kalman, Bobbie. *Invasive Animal Species.* New York, NY: Crabtree Publishing Company, 2016.

Spilsbury, Richard. *Invasive Species Underwater.* New York, NY: PowerKids Press, 2015.

Websites

Alien Invaders
dnr.wi.gov/org/caer/ce/eek/earth/aliens.htm
Find out about many more kinds of invasive species.

Invasive Species
nationalgeographic.org/encyclopedia/invasive-species/
Read more about invasive species and how they harm native habitats.

Publisher's note to educators and parents: Our editors have carefully reviewed these websites to ensure that they are suitable for students. Many websites change frequently, however, and we cannot guarantee that a site's future contents will continue to meet our high standards of quality and educational value. Be advised that students should be closely supervised whenever they access the Internet.

INDEX